Prayers
for Baby's
Christening

Written and compiled
by Lois Rock

Illustrated by Sanya Rescek

LION
CHILDREN'S

A christening is a gift of love.

*It shows the love of those who
make promises to guide a little child
in the way of faith.*

*It is also a celebration of the love of God,
who welcomes little children into the
kingdom of heaven.*

*The prayers in this book will keep alive
the promises made at the christening and
help a little one grow in faith.*

contents

God's love

The sun may shine
The rain may fall
God will always
Love us all.

Victoria Tebbs

God loves us

Thank you, dear God, for the
love between parent and child.

May the love of those we can
see and touch help us
understand the love of God.

Little baby,
just awakened,
you are part of
God's creation.

Little baby,
oh, so small,
God is father
of us all.

God cares for us

Dear God,
You clothe the flowers in lovely petals.
You provide food for the wild birds.
We see how much you care for these things
and remember that you care for us even more.

God, who made the earth,
The air, the sky, the sea,
Who gave the light its birth,
Careth for me.

God, who made the grass,
The flower, the fruit, the tree,
The day and night to pass,
Careth for me.

God, who made all things,
On earth, in air, in sea,
Who changing seasons brings,
Careth for me.

Sarah Betts Rhodes

We help one another

Dear God,
Thank you for the good-hearted people
who love us, help us and encourage us.

May we learn to love, to help and
to encourage others.

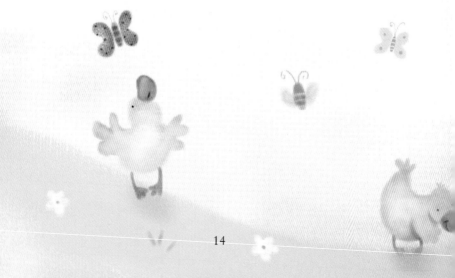

God bless all those that I love;
God bless all those that love me;
God bless all those that love those that I love,
and all those that love those that love me.

From an old New England sampler

God's creation

The trees grow down,
down into the earth,
right down into long ago.

The trees grow up,
up into the sky,
right up where the strong winds blow.

The trees, they sway,
they sway in the wind
and whisper a secret song:

'We thank you, God,
for keeping us safe,
that we might grow tall and strong.'

For sun
and showers,
for seeds
and flowers,
we give you thanks,
dear God.

All God's creatures

Think of the tiniest of little, tiny things.
Think of the hugest of huge, enormous things.
Imagine the God who made the tiny things.
Imagine the God who made the huge things.
Just imagine: the Maker God.

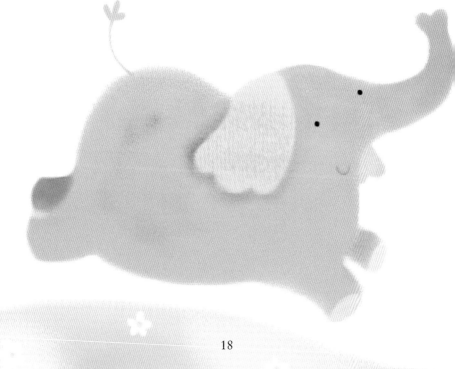

All things bright and beautiful,
All creatures great and small,
All things wise and wonderful,
The Lord God made them all.

Cecil Frances Alexander

Following Jesus

I'm learning to be more like Jesus,
I'm learning the right way to live.
I'm learning to show loving kindness,
I'm learning to truly forgive.

The Christmas Baby

Away in a manger, no crib for a bed,
The little Lord Jesus laid down his sweet head.
The stars in the bright sky
Looked down where he lay,
The little Lord Jesus asleep on the hay.

The cattle are lowing, the baby awakes,
But little Lord Jesus no crying he makes.
I love thee, Lord Jesus!
Look down from the sky,
And stay by my side until morning is nigh.

Be near me, Lord Jesus; I ask thee to stay
Close by me for ever, and love me, I pray.
Bless all the dear children in thy tender care,
And fit us for heaven, to live with thee there.

Traditional

22

23

The preacher from Galilee

When Jesus became a teacher, crowds came to listen to him.

'Set your hearts on living as God wants,' he told them. 'Do what is right and good. Then you will be part of God's kingdom.

'You can be sure that God will take care of you.'

From Matthew 6

One day, some mothers brought their children to Jesus. They wanted him to say a prayer for them.

'Let the children come to me and do not stop them,' he said. 'The kingdom of heaven belongs to such as these.'

From Matthew 19

Jesus, friend of little children,
Be a friend to me;
Take my hand, and ever keep me
Close to thee.

Walter J. Mathams

Jesus the storyteller

Jesus told this story:

'There was once a shepherd who had a hundred sheep.

'One day, he found he only had ninety-nine.

'He left the ninety-nine safely in the pasture and went to find his missing sheep.

'Over the hills he walked, along stony paths and past prickly thorns.

'At long last he heard a sound. "Baa, baa!"

'He was overjoyed. Gently he carried the forlorn creature home and put it safely with the flock.

'"Let's have a party," he said to his friends. "For my sheep was lost, and now it is found."

'God is like that shepherd,' said Jesus. 'When someone who has lost their way comes back into God's kingdom, all the angels sing for joy.'

Dear God, you are my shepherd,
You give me all I need,
You take me where the grass grows green
And I can safely feed.

You take me where the water
Is quiet and cool and clear;
And there I rest and know I'm safe
For you are always near.

From Psalm 23

Light for the world

'Listen,' said Jesus. 'Let your lives shine with goodness. Make the world a brighter place.'

From Matthew 5

Dear God,
Help me to brighten each and every day
with kindliness and cheerfulness.

May my life shine
like a star in the night,
filling my world
with goodness and light.

From Philippians 2:15

The prayer Jesus taught

Our Father in heaven,
hallowed be your name,
your kingdom come,
your will be done,
on earth as in heaven.
Give us today our daily bread.
Forgive us our sins
as we forgive those who sin against us.
Lead us not into temptation
but deliver us from evil.

For the kingdom, the power,
and the glory are yours
now and for ever.
Amen.

The Lord's Prayer

Blessings

Wherever you go,
May God the Father be with you.

Wherever you go,
May God the Son be with you.

Wherever you go,
May God the Spirit be with you.

Bless me and help me

May God's Spirit come
like the winds that blow:
make me good and wise;
help my faith to grow.

May God's Spirit come
like a flame of gold:
fill my life with joy;
make me strong and bold.

Dear God, bless me
and make me good
and help me do
the things I should.

Bless those I love

Bless my Dad,
so strong and tall:
the kindest Daddy
of them all.

God bless Mummy when we're together
and when we are far away;
God bless her when she's busy with work,
and please give her time to play.

Bless all the people who love me, dear God,
and bless all the people I love;
help us to help one another each day
and make earth like heaven above.

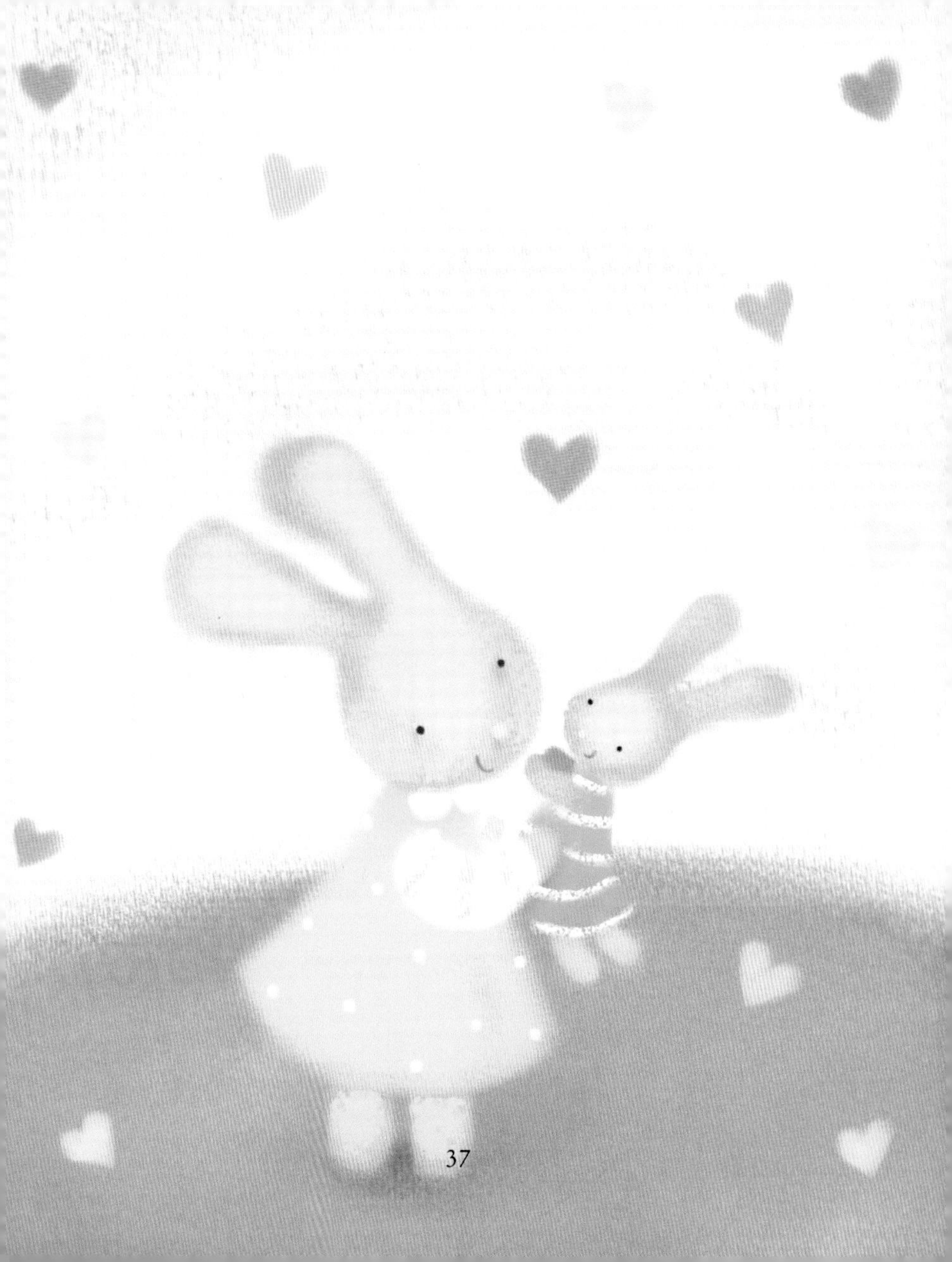

Bless each day

Bless the day, dear God,
from sunrise to sunset.
Bless the night, dear God,
from sunset to sunrise.

This new day is for living,
This new day is for giving;
This new day is for caring,
This new day is for sharing.

Bless this house

Bless the window
Bless the door
Bless the ceiling
Bless the floor
Bless this place which is our home
Bless us as we go and come.

Lord, make this house
a holy place
filled with your love
and heaven's grace.

Mealtime blessings

Thank you for the world so sweet
Thank you for the food we eat
Thank you for the birds that sing
Thank you, God, for everything.

Edith Rutter Leatham

Each time we eat,
may we remember God's love.

Prayer from China

Goodnight

Jesus, tender Shepherd, hear me,
Bless your little lamb tonight;
Through the darkness please be near me;
Keep me safe till morning light.

Mary Lundie Duncan

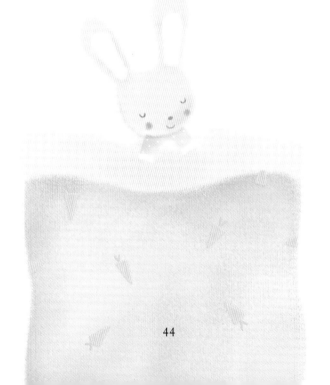

44

Lord, keep us safe this night,
Secure from all our fears;
May angels guard us while we sleep,
Till morning light appears.

John Leland

Now I lay me down to sleep,
I pray thee, Lord, thy child to keep;
Thy love to guard me through the night
And wake me in the morning light.

Traditional

I see the moon
And the moon sees me;
God bless the moon
And God bless me.

Traditional